SCHOLASTIC
News
Nonfiction Readers

Is It a Dinosaur?

by Susan H. Gray

Children's Press®
A Division of Scholastic Inc.
New York Toronto London Auckland Sydney
Mexico City New Delhi Hong Kong
Danbury, Connecticut

These content vocabulary word builders are for grades 1–2.

Subject Consultant: Rudyard W. Sadleir, Doctoral Candidate in Evolutionary Biology,
University of Chicago, Chicago, Illinois

Reading Consultant: Cecilia Minden-Cupp, PhD, Former Director of the Language and Literacy Program,
Harvard Graduate School of Education, Cambridge, Massachusetts

Photographs © 2007: Alamy Images: 7 (BananaStock), 20 top left (Bruce Coleman Inc.), 23 top right (Mike Danton), 12 (Nigel Reed), 5 top left, 17 bottom (Frances Roberts); Allan D. Smith/Fossilsmith Studios: cover top right, 20 top right; Corbis Images/Joe McDonald: 21 top left; Getty Images/Louie Psihoyos: 9; Natural History Museum, London/Michael Long: 2, 4 top, 17 top; Photo Researchers, NY: 21 top right, 23 bottom right (Chris Butler), cover bottom right, 23 bottom left (Chase Studio), 21 bottom left (W. Treat Davidson), back cover, 4 bottom left, 5 bottom right, 15, 18 (Francois Gohier), cover top left, 19, 20 bottom left (Roger Harris), 1, 5 bottom left, 11, 23 top left (Joe Tucciarone); The Image Works/Topham: cover bottom left, 4 bottom right, 13.
Illustrations by James E. Whitcraft

Book Design: Simonsays Design!
Book Production: The Design Lab

Library of Congress Cataloging-in-Publication Data
Gray, Susan Heinrichs.
  Is it a dinosaur? / by Susan H. Gray.
    p. cm. — (Scholastic news nonfiction readers)
  Includes bibliographical references and index.
  ISBN-13: 978-0-531-17486-9
  ISBN-10: 0-531-17486-7
  1. Dinosaurs—Juvenile literature. I. Title. II. Series.
  QE861.5G745 2006
  567.9—dc22   2006024041

1 2 3 4 5 6 7 8 9 10 R 16 15 14 13 12 11 10 09 08 07

CONTENTS

WORD HUNT

Look for these words as you read. They will be in **bold**.

armored
(**ar**-murd)

pelycosaur
(**pel**-uh-kuh-sawr)

plesiosaur
(**plee**-see-uh-sawr)

4

glyptodont
(**glip**-tuh-dont)

hollow
(**hol**-oh)

pterosaur
(**tehr**-uh-sawr)

skeleton
(**skell**-uh-tuhn)

WHAT WE KNOW

We know a lot about dinosaurs. They were four-legged land animals. They couldn't fly. They didn't live underwater. The oldest ones lived 220 million years ago. The newest ones died out 65 million years ago.

Museums are good places to learn about dinosaurs.

Let's go on a hunt to find out even more about dinosaurs.

We'll look at fossil bones from all over the world.

But will they all be from dinosaurs? Let's find out!

A museum worker prepares dinosaur bones for an exhibit.

Here are some arm and hand bones. They are **hollow** and light. Each hand has one very long finger. Are they dinosaur bones?

No, these can't be dinosaur bones. They came from a flying animal and dinosaurs didn't fly. They came from a **pterosaur**.

hollow

Some pterosaurs had a wingspan of more than 50 feet (15 meters)!

This animal was longer than a bus! It could not fly. Instead of arms and legs, it had flippers. Is it a dinosaur?

No! Dinosaurs didn't have flippers. These must be the bones of a swimming animal—a **plesiosaur**.

flipper

Plesiosaurs lived in the ocean and ate fish.

13

These are the bones of a huge animal with sharp teeth. It did not fly or swim. It lived 290 million years ago. Do you think it was a dinosaur?

If you said no, you are correct! There were no dinosaurs 290 million years ago. This animal was a **pelycosaur**.

Dimetrodon was one kind of pelycosaur.

These remains came from an **armored** animal. It lived a few thousand years ago. What do you think? Was it a dinosaur?

The dinosaurs died out millions of years earlier. So these can't be dinosaur bones. These bones came from a **glyptodont**.

Glyptodonts looked a lot like huge armadillos!

These bones belonged to a huge land animal. It lived during the time of the dinosaurs. It had no wings or flippers. Hooray! We found a dinosaur **skeleton**!

skeleton

Triceratops was a large, plant-eating dinosaur with three horns on its head.

WHICH ONE IS A DINOSAUR?

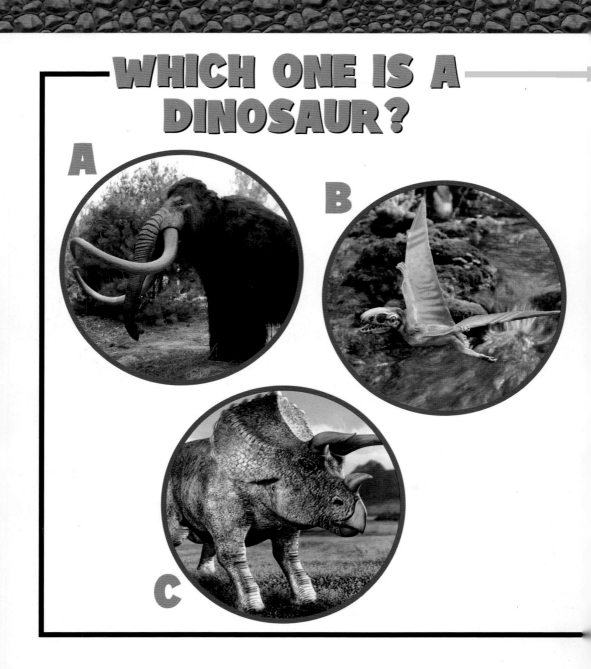

A

B

C

D

E

F

Answer: C

21

YOUR NEW WORDS

armored (**ar**-murd) covered with armor such as plates, head shields, or a hard shell

glyptodont (**glip**-tuh-dont) an animal with armor on its head and back

hollow (**hol**-oh) not solid; having an empty space inside

pelycosaur (**pel**-uh-kuh-sawr) an animal that lived long before the dinosaurs

plesiosaur (**plee**-see-uh-sawr) a large, swimming animal that was related to the dinosaurs

pterosaur (**tehr**-uh-sawr) a flying animal that was related to the dinosaurs

skeleton (**skell**-uh-tuhn) the entire set of the bones of an animal

MORE DINOSAURS

Allosaurus

Brachiosaurus

Parasaurolophus

Tyrannosaurus

FIND OUT MORE

Book:

Barrett, Paul. *National Geographic Dinosaurs*. National Geographic Children's Books, 2001.

Website:

ZoomDinosaurs.com
www.enchantedlearning.com/subjects/dinosaurs

MEET THE AUTHOR

Susan H. Gray has a master's degree in zoology. She has written more than seventy science and reference books for children. She especially loves to write about animals. Susan and her husband, Michael, live in Cabot, Arkansas.